Message For My Readers

"A journey of a thousand miles must begin with a single step."
— Lao Tzu

Dedication

To my gorgeous wife who loved me even when I was overweight and unhealthy.

And for those who want to improve quality of their lives.

Huge Thank You and Words of Gratitude!

"As we express our gratitude, we must never forget that the highest appreciation is not to utter words, but to live"
- John F. Kennedy

First and foremost, Thank You for downloading this book. At the end of the day I'm **extremely** grateful for **every** download and **every** purchase. It really makes me smile and motivates me. I wish that every person would put their best forward for the human race. I wish you unlimited mental strength and discipline to achieve your goals and dreams. **Together** we can make the difference.

If you found the information useful I would be extremely grateful if you could write a short Amazon review. It really does make the difference and I personally read every review and take notes. I want to improve my books, so that I can provide more value to other people. I know that my future books will give you the best experience possible.

Table Of Contents

Workout Buddy – Yes or No?

Make The most of Your time. Workout partner is good once in a while.

This chapter may not apply to all but I'm sure it will apply to some. Personally, I used to think it would be great to have a workout buddy. Someone I could talk with while working out, someone to keep me accountable in doing my workouts. There's no point in writing "Fancy" introduction, it's time to get serious!

Unfortunately what I found was that I was using half my energy talking and couldn't perform my exercises with the same intensity as I could when I was alone.

I believe it boils down to these factors. These factors may apply more to women but I've personally seen guys doing the same thing. One factor is that we are social creatures. When we get to work-out, chances are it may have been a week or more since we've seen our friend. Everyone has a busy life and busy schedules. So you're likely to spend a lot of time during that workout chatting and playing catchup. Not to say that you can't workout while talking. But I've personally found I can't perform as well because I'm not concentrating on my reps and form when I'm talking about the events of the past week. It's very hard to multi-task in that sense.

A second factor is that we may be dependent on our friend's schedule if we want to worko-ut together. What can then happen is that if they cancel on our usual workout day, we are most likely to bail out on our workout as well. We have fallen into that habit of having to have a workout buddy to keep us motivated and we can't summon up the ability to motivate ourselves to do our workout. And if they cancel again, guess what? You've likely missed two workouts in a row. That can really set you back. Working out is all about consistency.

A third factor is that we may be somewhat self-conscious doing our workouts in front of someone else. I know personally **I** am. If I'm at the gym doing my own thing, I don't usually care what others may think about that weird squat move I'm trying to do. I don't know them and they don't know me. But if a friend were there with me I would definitely feel self-conscious about it. I most likely would skip that exercise and maybe a few others. Before you know it your planned workout (and you now know why you need to plan workouts!) has no plan at all.

I'm definitely not suggesting to never workout with a buddy. Sometimes it's imperative to have a spotter when lifting heavy weights for instance. But I am suggesting to consider working out solo. You may find you like it more and enjoy your workouts because it's about "ME" time. I personally love blasting music from my headphones in my

ears while I do my thing. It's a little harder to get motivated when I can't listen to my tunes because

Share Your Success with the Others

Let people know your

goals and don't forget to let them know when

you achieve

them!

One thing that will definitely motivate you and keep you accountable is to publicly announce your goals. Tell your friends and family of course. I believe any goal that you have will be strengthened with the love and support of friends and family. This network (even if it is a network of one) can be very important in helping you achieve the results you want. The supportive people in your life will continue to love and cherish you no matter what the outcome is. This takes the pressure and stress off of us to better perform without anxiety holding us back.

On the other hand, publicly announcing it via social media can also be a huge motivator in the opposite way. By publicly posting your goals via a tweet, a blog post, a video or other social media channel it can hold you accountable. That announcement was made in WRITING. If you post to your followers you certainly don't want to let them down, do you? You would rather be an inspiration to others. Showing them how if you could do it, anyone can do it!

Say your goal is to lose five pounds. I would suggest that at every pound lost you make an announcement about it. You might think, oh who cares, it's only one stinking pound? But others will be inspired and will voice their support. They will see you making progress and will want to help support your journey. This support will help motivate you to continue your progress and reach your ultimate goal!

Some workout apps even have sharing tools. Once you've completed the exercise you can share it to your social media communities, proudly showing that you did it!

Feel The Power of The Music

Choose sounds that will motivate you!

This chapter resonates with me the most. Nothing else seems to have as much power to get me motivated and off my arse as much as music does. It's currently helping me at this very moment to write this chapter. My brain is stimulated by it. I'm sure you've heard music described as "ear candy".

That's exactly what I think of it. Slightly addicting. You always want more. You're never satisfied with just one (song). Music has to the power to alter your mood just like that. When I don't *feel* like working out I tend to play some positive, upbeat, bass driven music. And I'm telling you play it LOUD. Whether you have headphones on or can listen in your car. Just play it loud. It not only gets me going pre-workout, I feel that I have a better workout just because I'm listening to music while I work out. I've been stuck at the gym a few times without my headphones or mp3 player and the workout process just didn't feel the same.

Think about how you could be in a downright rotten mood. You're flipping radio stations or shuffling songs on your mobile device. You're glaring at other drivers on the road or perhaps for some saying some choice words aloud. Suddenly one of your favorite songs comes on. Ever notice how that rotten mood disappears as you bob your head, sing along and forget all that stress and negativity behind?

I think this is one of the most often overlooked motivators when it comes to working out. I feel like working out just by listening to certain songs regardless if I have already done my workout for the day! Try to keep it varied. If you feel really pumped up for a week listening to the same pre-workout song, great. But don't rely on that one song in case next week you're suddenly tired of that song and all of a sudden it doesn't motivate you anymore.

I'm constantly searching for new music to uplift and inspire me. YouTube is a great source for that. So many great channels have uploaded one hour or longer playlists of multiple tracks. These work for me much better than me trying to create my own playlists as I'm lazy in that aspect! Plus, I don't waste time searching around on my inp3 player looking for the next song to play. My mind stays focused and concentrated on my workout.

Have a Plan

Set Goals. Prepare a workout plan. Or Buy it From a Personal Trainer.

With most things in life, it's best to have a plan. Nothing could be even more true for your workouts. I've found myself wandering around the gym too many times trying to figure out what I want to do. Not knowing what machines to use, not knowing what muscles to work. Feeling like I'm wasting my time because of indecision. All because I didn't have a plan of what I wanted to accomplish during that workout.

I would highly suggest writing down what you want to do the night before if you work out in the mornings. If you work out in the evenings write it out during the day, maybe on a lunch break. I think this accomplishes three things. One, it prepares your mind for your workout. You have put forth the effort of writing it down. This subconsciously tells your mind that it must be important enough to actually accomplish and get done. Two, it helps you have a more focused and intense workout because you are not wasting time wandering around aimlessly trying to decide what to do during your workout. Three, it helps you achieve your goals in **a much more** proactive fashion. If your goal was to drop five pounds and get a flatter stomach, wouldn't it be beneficial you think to spend time doing core exercises and cardio training? If you have your plan in place you know what needs to get done to achieve the results.

I'm just starting to get into writing things down myself. For a long time, I would plan out my workout in my head. I would think, ok I did biceps and triceps yesterday, I'm going to do back and shoulders today. I have a fairly decent memory so it worked for me. However, I have begun writing what I want to accomplish for those times when your brain isn't awake yet or when your brain is too fried to remember what the heck you were planning earlier in the day. It greatly helps me to just quickly look at the notes I save on my phone in case I have a memory blank.

If things are feeling dull in your workouts and you're tired of doing the same exercises, mix it up. I try to do something a little different each time. I may do the popular 10 minute workout and do two rounds for a quick crunch workout. Then the next time I may lift weights and throw punches at my punching bag. The next time I do weights I may jump rope in between sets. There are too many books, videos, and resources out there to get bored with working out.

Importance of Proper Nutrition

This chapter may seem like a no-brainer but I wanted to include it to stress the importance of how eating right can help you stay motivated. Nobody who is on a downward spiraling sugar crash feels like going to exercise and pump some weights.

Throughout my years of being concerned for my fitness I have definitely learned it is easier to eat the right foods and have a sustainable amount of energy than to eat the wrong foods and try to go burn off those calories. The times I have worked out after eating junk food, potato chips, highly processed frozen dinners and the like have been the hardest times to muster up my motivation.

I'm not saying don't cut out all of your favorite foods and live miserably. I certainly didn't do it that way. What I am saying is to eat those sugary, chocolaty, fattening foods in a very moderate way. Like once a week, treat yourself to very small servings of whatever is your vice. That way you won't binge on them during the week. It is important to make sure you drink a TON of water every day. I don't think people really understand how much you should be drinking. Water will help flush out the toxins in your body. Next up, good old fruits and vegetables. Since I'm a morning workout person I sometimes like to have a glass of water and a small piece of fruit before beginning. This gives my body some energy to perform. Natural sugar in fruit is the good kind, learn to love it!

My other advice is for meals, have 3/4 of your plate be meat and veggies. If you're vegetarian or vegan or any other variation in between, just find ways to add protein into your meal other than meat. The protein will satisfy you and keep you from other cravings. The other 1/4 of your plate could be a carb. I know I love my pasta, potatoes, and rice. I've just learned to scale it back to keep me from feeling bloated, to sleep better, and have a more clear and alert mind. Oh yeah, and to stay motivated with my workouts!

Change Your Workout Time

Change Your Workout time if You are feeling down.

This is a pretty easy concept to grasp. You may think you hate working out, hate getting up early in the morning to fit in a workout. Or if you currently workout in the evenings you may be feeling too burned out after work to put in a good session.

I have great news because this has happened personally to me. Except for when I went to the gym in college, I mostly did my workouts in the evenings after work. I thought, I don't want to get up any earlier so I'll just workout after work. It will help relieve stress and all that jazz. Most days I had to drag myself to the gym or outside for a run. It was really hard to muster up the extra energy after working 8-io hours a day. I would squeeze in one good workout on the morning. One day I thought, I've got to mix this up.

Evening workouts just aren't benefiting me and I'm not getting the increased energy I should be getting. I decided I wanted to get up earlier, workout, and have long-lasting energy that sustained me through the day

The great news is it has been working for me! It may be

the complete opposite for you if you are definitely not a morning person. You may be forcing yourself to the gym kicking and screaming all the way. My point is simply this. TRY SWITCHING IT UP. If you're doing it one way and are not happy and not feeling motivated, try it the other way. You may be pleasantly surprised. I certainly didn't think I wanted to get up any earlier than I already was for the weekday. But what I found out was my body actually looked forward to it. My eyes were opening before my alarm clock went off and my body was looking forward to the day long energy it was going to receive from completing a morning workout.

Another benefit about switching my workout schedule to the mornings was that I enjoyed making myself my favorite green smoothie for breakfast. I never made smoothies after my workouts before when they were in the evenings because I was typically eating dinner right after.

FREQUENCY

Be frequent in your workouts. Make sure you get enough of them in a week but have at least a day off to

rest.

Frequency is VERY important. You cannot follow the above mentioned tips without keeping a consistent workout schedule. The amount of time and how many days you work-out in a week can easily vary from person to person. Make sure you are medically fit before entering a workout program.

Obviously if you are training intensely to complete a marathon or enter a bodybuilding competition you are going to have a different workout plan than someone just trying to lose 5 pounds.

It's hard to stay motivated though if you are not working out enough times a week. Personally I strive for three to four days a week. Eventually I'd like to push myself harder and go for four to five days a week. Schedule it on your calendar. Decide what days are easiest for you and make sure it's more than twice a week. I believe doing a workout fewer than three times a week will make it very hard to sustain the progress you've made. You have to keep building upon that. Give your body rest but not for too long

On the opposite side of the spectrum, I do believe you can work-out too much. I think everyone needs at least one full day of rest per week. I still think you can go for a walk or a light jog that day but otherwise no intense workouts or training should be performed on rest day.

One final tip that helps me stay frequent and intentional about my workouts is to think it over in my head the night before.

I have it written down what I'm going to do and then I sort of meditate on it before I go to sleep. It is one of the last things on my mind before sleeping and thus it's one of the first upon waking.

Conclusion

If you find this book helpful and worth the value you've purchased it for, please do leave an accurate feedback of the book, this will help me improving the book and it will reaching more people as well as helping others deciding whether they find it to be the right one for them.

It's been an honorable journey serving you and providing you with what's necessary for you to grow and expand beyond your current limits and challenges.

Take action and live the life you truly deserve, it's simple, it's not easy changing your life, it takes dedication, if you're meant to succeed, you will, because the mind translates your values and standards into a reality.

- George Griffith